W9-CBI-166

Library of Congress Cataloging-in-Publication Data:
Laffon, Martine.
[Livre des comment. English]
The book of how / Martine Laffon, Hortense de Chabaneix.
p. cm.
ISBN-13: 978-0-8109-0716-4
ISBN-10: 0-8109-0716-X
1. Questions and answers—Juvenile literature. I. De Chabaneix, Hortense.
II. Title.
AG195.L324 2006
031.02—dc22
2006014835

Text copyright © 2005 Editions de la Martinière, Paris
English translation copyright © 2007 Harry N. Abrams, Inc.

Translated by Gita Daneshjoo
Originally published in French as *Le Livre des Comment*
in 2005 by Editions de la Martinière Jeunesse

Published in 2007 by Abrams Books for Young Readers, an imprint of Harry N. Abram
Inc. All rights reserved. No portion of this book may be reproduced, stored in a retrie
system, or transmitted in any form or by any means, mechanical, electronic, photocopy
recording, or otherwise, without written permission from the publisher.

Printed and bound in France
10 9 8 7 6 5 4 3 2 1

HNA ▌▌▌▌▌
harry n. abrams, inc.
a subsidiary of La Martinière Groupe
115 West 18th Street
New York, NY 10011
www.hnabooks.com

The Book of How

Martine Laffon
Hortense de Chabaneix

Illustrations by
Jacques Azam

Abrams Books for Young Readers
New York

Contents

How can you tell when you're a grown-up?

When I'm a grown-up, I can do what I want! As you get older, the need to be independent and make your own decisions can be so urgent you'd do almost anything to enter the world of adults. But at what point in life are you considered a grown-up? Is it only a question of age?

In traditional cultures, such as those in Africa, young people must prove their courage, responsibility, strength, and respect for the values of the community before they can be considered an adult.

But becoming a grown-up is not only a matter of turning a certain age. You also have to act the part of an adult by behaving yourself and not acting out or foolishly following a whim. The qualities and values we learn as children are the keys to becoming an adult. But this doesn't happen overnight! After all, in life, you never really stop growing . . .

In the past, certain cultural rites of passage marked the end of adolescence and the initiation into adulthood. Even today, each young person slowly goes through a series of important, life-changing events.

The age at which one enters adulthood has varied over the years, depending on the time period and the country of origin. Nowadays, in the United States, you're considered an adult at eighteen: at this age, a person can vote and participate in society as a legal citizen.

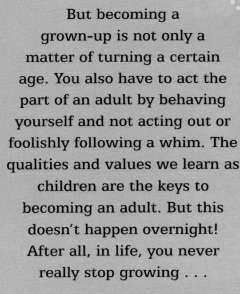

How do you catch a cold?

A long time ago, people thought that being exposed to cold weather could result in a cold. Thankfully, our bodies aren't hat fragile. Nevertheless, during colder months, we stay inside more, making it easier to spread viruses from one person to another.

I'm the cold virus!

First I'll cause a little nasal swelling...

then I'll hit the bronchial tubes!

Ha!

The most common cold virus is from the rhinovirus family. This virus plants itself and multiplies in the nasal cavity, causing inflammation, which results in runny noses and sneezing. These viruses are spread through the air, and are very contagious.

Each time you cough or yawn without covering your mouth, lay your tissue around carelessly, or spit, you run the risk of contaminating the people around you. Some countries, such as Japan, have very strict civil conduct laws: a person with a cold can't go out in public without covering his or her nose and mouth with a surgical mask!

Even though we can't change other people's personal habits, we can still take certain precautions to build up our resistance to infection. Eating healthy food gives us the vitamins and energy necessary to protect ourselves from viruses. Sleeping well is also helpful, because fatigue prevents us from properly defending our bodies from illness.

You should never hesitate to open the windows of your room, classroom, or anywhere else you might find yourself indoors. This way, you can be sure that the air keeps circulating!

How does my foot fall asleep?

Did you ever feel like your foot was stuffed with pins and needles? Everyone has experienced this funny feeling at least once in life!

Basically, pins and needles appear as a result of the way our body's blood circulates. Each time we cross our legs or keep them bent uncomfortably for too long, it squashes our nerves and temporarily slows the circulation of blood in that area.

But your body's heart still beats regularly and the blood flows normally elsewhere in your body, causing a traffic jam! Think of a sand castle at the beach: even though we try to protect it with barriers, sooner or later, the waves come crashing through!

When you uncross your legs or change position, all that blood waiting to circulate engulfs the veins with such force that it irritates our nerve endings and causes an uncomfortable prickly sensation, like a bunch of pins and needles are coursing through your foot.

That stings!

Until normal circulation is restored, there's not much you can do about it: massaging it, dancing around, or jumping up and down like a grasshopper won't make it go away any faster!

How does a giant ocean liner float?

Isn't it strange that a 50,000-ton tanker floats in the ocean, but a marble sinks in the bathtub?

Archimedes realized how to resolve this enigma while taking a bath. He came out of it crying "Eureka!" (Greek for "I've found it!") He discovered that his body weighed less inside the water than out, as though he was "lifted" by the water. This force exerted by the water on the body is now called Archimedes' Principle.

A ball filled with glass weighs more than a normal ball filled with water, so it sinks. An ocean liner filled with air weighs less than an ocean liner filled with water, so it floats! A crown made of gold and silver weighs less than a crown made of pure gold, so it takes less time to sink. This is how Archimedes was able to prove to the king that he had been cheated!

To explain this phenomenon, you have to go back to Greece around 250 B.C. At that time, Hiero, the king of Syracuse, suspected a goldsmith of having swindled him by secretly mixing silver with the gold for his crown. He asked his favorite mathematician, Archimedes, to prove the fraud without damaging the jewel.

When an object is placed in water, it displaces the water, causing the water to rise. The force on an object submerged in water is equal to the weight of the water displaced by the object. If the object is lighter than the displaced water, it floats, because the displaced water has the force necessary to keep the object afloat. But if the object is heavier, it sinks. An object floats as long as its weight is lighter than if it were submerged in water.

Archimedes, stop doing math in the bathtub!

How do people think in **foreign** languages?

Words can take on a life of their own. Words are filled with noises, colors, odors, feelings, and emotions . . . a colorful palette that draws on one's experience and imagination, and gives them meaning.

Learning to think in another language is not a matter of simply memorizing new vocabulary. One must also live among native speakers of the language, and discover their culture firsthand. How do they express their feelings? What makes them laugh?

It has been said that people who live in the Artic have at least thirty words for snow, taking into account its color, shape, the sound it makes under a sled or the hooves of reindeer, and its fragility. As for nomadic Mongols, they draw upon an extensive vocabulary for describing horse-breeding, a subject in which they have great expertise.

You can think in another language the day it becomes so familiar that you stop depending on your first language to translate what you want to say.

How can you avoid setting the table?

Annoying tasks have a way of repeating themselves. No matter how many excuses you come up with—a telephone call, an urgent homework assignment, or any other pressing activity—there's no escaping one of the world's worst chores: setting the table!

Though you may secretly wish that you could eat sandwiches every day of the week, or dine on paper plates, that's not going to happen. So you may as well try to change your attitude about setting the table.

Start by using your imagination: tell yourself how important it is for the family to share their meal together. Or take on the role of the model child: Are Mom and Dad exhausted after a long day at work? Maybe I should give them a hand!

You can even adopt a more communal attitude: the house belongs to all of us, and we all must try to contribute in every way we can. If you're still not convinced, try some math: four forks plus four knives, four glasses, and four plates equals what? Then calculate the total number of tableware items you've set in one year!

If this still doesn't do the trick, maybe you'd like an adventure: next time you set the table, use chopsticks instead of silverware, old newspapers instead of placemats, and coconut shells in place of plates; set the table on the floor and pass around cushions for people to sit on. And if you're feeling more romantic, why not dine by candlelight . . .

The more you distract yourself with fun ideas, the faster you'll set the table! Doesn't it feel good to finish your chores?

How do you know when you're happy?

Is it possible to be 100 percent sure that you're happy? As sure as $2 + 2 = 4$? No! There's no such thing as a happiness test. It's a personal feeling, the kind of fulfillment you get by spending quality time in nature or bonding with other people.

Do you have to be rich, powerful, famous, or in love to be happy? Not really. Wealth can disappear overnight, power can be lost, and fame can easily fade!

Wise people believe that we're responsible for our own happiness, and that happiness depends solely on us and not on our life circumstances. Being happy means renouncing the pleasures and desires that would only result in fleeting happiness. Instead, one must achieve tranquility of the mind and body, which is what true happiness is all about.

Other people think that happiness can only be achieved when you make others happy. After all, they argue, how can I be happy when others suffer?

There are plenty of theories on "how to attain happiness." But there is no one formula that can guarantee it. Don't spend too much time trying to find it, or you just might end up unhappy!

How do boats fit into bottles?

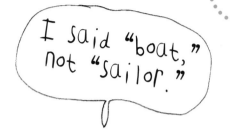

I said "boat," not "sailor."

Are there really tiny little sailors on tiny little boats who sail into tiny little bottles in the sea? Or are there special machines that can form-fit bottles around certain objects?

The answer to both questions is no! To fit a boat into a bottle, you must first choose any old bottle and measure it: its length and width, as well as the diameter of its neck. Next, you must design the boat to fit the bottle's dimensions, just like any object in reduced scale.

The boats found in bottles have some unique characteristics: their masts can be folded in order to fit into the bottle's neck, and by a simple pull of a string, open into place inside the bottle itself.

In the beginning of the nineteenth century, a time of rapid industrial development, glass bottles were produced in vast quantities and became popular items of consumption in markets around the world.

Shortly thereafter, idle sailors at sea and lonely lighthouse keepers came up with the idea of turning these bottles into picture windows! Today, thousands of model-boat bottlers around the world keep the traditions of these old navigators alive.

How can a **carrot** make you happy?

In the days of antiquity, Greeks and Romans were familiar with the therapeutic uses of carrots. However, the reddish-orange root vegetable that we know today was more purplish—nearly black—back then, and hard as a rock. They ate them anyway, and extolled (without an explanation) their numerous health benefits.

Carotene is a pigment that the body converts to vitamin A. Vitamin A plays an important role in the body. For example, vitamin A helps slow the aging of skin cells and naturally protects us from the sun's rays.

Whether or not you like carrots, the moment you bite into one you should think of all its great properties: it gives you rosy cheeks, helps you see in the dark, and makes you feel happy.

Even Charlemagne was convinced of the carrot's many benefits. He advised all the monasteries of his empire to add carrots to their soup. Nowadays, carrots, or the carotene contained in them, are a recommended part of one's daily diet.

That's why carrots give us a good complexion. Vitamin A also helps regenerate cells in our liver. People with liver problems are often sad, and suffer from bad moods. By recommending that they eat carrots, not only can they get better, but they can also improve their attitude. By now I think you got the message: if you want to be healthy and happy, eat carrots everyday!

Eat your carrots!

How can a person eat insects?

Parents teach their children what to eat and what not to eat: they make distinctions between healthy food and junk food. Taste is learned and passed down according to culture. Although we may think that insects are gross and scary, some cultures find them tasty, and a major source of protein!

Figuring out what's edible, knowing how to cook it, and eating it all require a taste education, which is different for everyone. For children in Burkina Faso, the worms that live in the country's karite trees beginning in May are a real treat. They call it the "caviar of the bush," and there are lots of recipes for how to prepare it— baked or fried!

Crickets, locusts, grasshoppers, and caterpillars are also consumed in Asia, Africa, and South America.

Dinner is served!

bzzz
bzzz
bzzz

But be careful! To practice entomophagy (the eating of insects), you must learn how to differentiate between insects you can eat and those you can't. For example, you should never eat ladybugs, bedbugs, or cockroaches: they're all toxic!

How were castles built without cranes?

People have always had more ideas than they have had strength to carry them out. Since people first began cultivating the land, we have used of all kinds of animals to make up for our physical limitations, and we've invented machines to do the heavy lifting.

To build castles, workers had to transport large blocks of stone to construction sites using baskets or wheelbarrows pulled by mules, horses, or cattle. Once the stones were cut to size, they were placed side by side and fused together using a mixture of lime, sand, and grout.

They left enough space between the stones to insert giant beams on which planks were nailed and pulleys attached. This wooden structure is the precursor to the scaffolding used in construction today. Masons and carpenters were able to build upward and lift even the heaviest stones using a pulley system.

Once the walls were constructed, the scaffolding was taken down, and the workers continued to the next building.

Nowadays, the highest buildings in the world take less than a year to build. In the Middle Ages, however, a castle or a cathedral often required several generations of artisans and nearly a century to build.

Come on, guys, move this stone.

Um... let's think about it for a few minutes.

17

How did someone know that **chocolate** tasted so good?

According to legend, Quetzalcoatl, the "feathered serpent" and god of civilization, taught the Mayans and the Aztecs, two groups indigenous to ancient Mexico, how to cultivate wild cocoa by extracting it from cocoa beans.

These cocoa beans were crushed in a mortar, and then roasted. The resulting pulp was blended with spices, chili peppers, cinnamon, and aniseed, then thinned out with water. Because cocoa beans are naturally bitter, the Aztecs added honey to the mixture to sweeten its taste.

The Aztec emperor Montezuma II served this beverage, "xocolatl," while welcoming the Spaniard Hernán Cortés to his land in 1519.

Chocolate made its appearance in the French court in 1615, when Anne of Austria, the daughter of the king of Spain, married King Louis XIII of France. Chocolate quickly became popular among the aristocratic classes.

It wasn't until the brutal Spanish conquest of Mexico that the Europeans discovered chocolate. The Spaniards modified the original recipe by replacing the chili pepper with vanilla beans and adding orange flower. Soon thereafter, they began drinking it hot, and learned to solidify it into tablets for easier transport.

Nowadays, although we no longer thank Quetzalcoatl for his divine offering, everyone knows that chocolate is good for the spirit!

How can I stop myself from getting angry?

It comes from nowhere. A bit of impatience, some annoyance, the tension builds, and, suddenly, it explodes!

Anger often arises when we simply can't achieve something that should be within our reach. Basically, it's the result of frustration. Anger makes our heart beat faster, our hormones rage, and our body temperature soar. Just like that! Once it starts, there's little you can do to stop it, short of taking a cold shower! The worst part is that anger not only tires you out but also leaves you feeling empty and depressed.

Though it may be difficult to control anger, the best tactic is to try to prevent it from spiraling out of control: learn to breathe deeply, for example, and also to talk about it. Even if you might not agree with someone, it doesn't have to lead to a heated argument. You can express your disagreement and still listen to another's position. This is what healthy debate is all about, and it's a necessary part of life.

The next time your parents tell you to go take your evening bath when you're in the middle of doing something else, instead of throwing a tantrum and yelling "Wait five minutes!" or "But why!?" and "You stink!", look them directly in the eyes and use your powers of self-control to calmly explain how you feel. You never know, it just might work! And if it doesn't? Go take your bath!

How should you respond to violence?

Is it wise to respond to violence with more violence? To attack others because they attacked you? Is there another solution?

Gandhi, the wise Indian leader, once declared, "An eye for an eye makes the whole world blind." Gandhi didn't tolerate injustice or conflict. He believed that the only way to eliminate injustice in the world was to fight it using nonviolent means.

Demonstrations, strikes, and discussions are nonviolent ways to publicly denounce injustice in the world. Martin Luther King, Jr., in the United States and Nelson Mandela in South Africa fought against racial segregation following Gandhi's nonviolent example.

All forms of violence, rape, and aggression must be denounced. Keeping quiet about it is, essentially, a way of condoning it. Whether you're a victim of or witness to violence, it's possible that you might hesitate to denounce the attackers for fear of revenge. But isn't it better to let justice handle it?

If you are mistreated at school, for example, why not talk about it with a teacher, a class representative, or the principal? Any kind of aggressive act that puts a person in danger is illegal. So when violence of any form occurs, don't hesitate to file a formal complaint to the police, alone or accompanied by an adult.

Should I use my little muscles or not???

How do you become a genius?

Being a genius means discovering or creating something so original that it changes the world.

In the past, geniuses weren't often seen in public because it was thought that their godlike minds could radically alter the destiny of those who crossed their paths.

As beliefs and traditions slowly evolved, a genius was viewed as a sort of hero with magical powers. Nowadays, the status of genius is conferred upon people with extraordinary skills and ability.

But becoming a genius doesn't happen in a day; it requires effort. For example, even if a child is born with an extremely quantitative mind, he'll never become a genius in math if he doesn't learn to count! Thomas Edison, the great inventor, said that genius was "one percent inspiration and ninety-nine percent perspiration."

No matter how much talent we're born with, we still have to work hard, because becoming a genius requires a great wealth of knowledge. If you don't apply yourself, study hard, and master various techniques, your natural talent may be wasted.

History books hail the numerous individuals who have contributed to the evolution of art, science, and philosophy. Yet some of those individuals lived miserable lives. Passion and talent combined with lifelong work don't necessarily result in fame and fortune. Today's world is full of unknown geniuses. You never know! Perhaps you, too, may be considered a genius someday.

I'm a genius!

Me too!

Me too!

Same here!

21

How can I meet my soul mate?

"One day my prince will come and whisper words of love in my ear . . ." Storybooks are full of handsome, brave, and wealthy princes who gallantly pursue poor princesses. Their valiance and determination are proof of true love. It's an irresistible idea!

Fairy tales speak to our greatest fears and desires: the fear of never finding love and the desire to fall in love and live happily ever after. Fairy tales depict a fantasy shared by all people, but they shouldn't be viewed as a guide on how to achieve happiness.

That's why you shouldn't wait around for your ideal mate in life to come along, like Prince Charming in a fairy tale.

There's nothing wrong with dreaming of a great love story. But beware of being disappointed by reality! You can't simply ask someone to become your childhood hero or heroine; that's not who they are, and that's not what love is.

Don't wait for your soul mate to come along. That's the same as chasing after something that doesn't exist. Be open to any encounter that comes your way. After all, love arrives when you least expect it!

How does a baby breathe in its mother's womb?

When a baby is in its mother's womb, it doesn't breathe like you or me. And although it's floating in fluid, it doesn't breathe like a fish in water, either.

A fetus's lungs start to develop around the sixth week of pregnancy and become functional around the eighth month. During the last months of pregnancy, a greasy substance is produced to protect the fetus's lungs and prevent them from filling up with liquid. Human lungs are designed to absorb air, and nothing else.

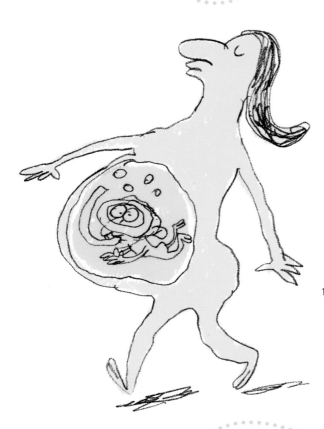

Although babies' lungs start to function once they're born, their lungs still exhibit respiratory activity in the womb. The umbilical cord attached to the mother contains two arteries and one vein. The vein transports oxygen and nutrients necessary for the fetus's development. The arteries transport carbon dioxide and waste back to the mother. This oxygen/carbon dioxide exchange is what we call breathing.

When the umbilical cord is cut at birth, the newborn must learn to live without its mother's help. In just a few seconds, its lungs open up, its blood flow quickens, and its body is ready to start functioning on its own. That's what I call a miracle!

How were fairy tales written?

Fairy tales were most likely written to address people's fear of the unknown. Lightning, thunderstorms, and the disappearance of the sun at sunset and its reappearance at dawn seem less frightening when we give them an explanation, even an imaginary one.

Aren't volcanic eruptions less scary when we pretend that they are caused by an underground giant suffering from indigestion? If you live in Japan, where there are frequent earthquakes, isn't it reassuring to imagine that the tremors are caused by a giant jumping from island to island?

Our need to dream and transform everyday occurrences into spectacular events is another explanation for fairy tales. In the real world, the strong often defeat the weak and the poor almost never get rich overnight.

But anything can happen in the magical world of fairy tales. Cinderella, the poor mistreated girl condemned to a life of housework, meets her Prince Charming. Little Tom Thumb endures a series of misadventures, including getting kidnapped, before uniting with his family. In fairy tales, standard roles are reversed! The weak triumph over the strong and live happily ever after.

Let me tell you a story!

Even though various details may differ from culture to culture, fairy tale themes are universal.

25

How are fireworks made?

It's my secret recipe!

Long ago, in China, bamboo was thrown in the fire to scare off Nian, a fierce monster that, according to legend, descended hungrily on villages in search of food. The bamboo exploded in the fire, creating a loud crackling noise, and causing the evil Nian to flee. This custom may be the origin of modern-day fireworks.

In any case, it was the Chinese who invented the first chemical explosives by combining sulfur, charcoal, and saltpeter. This mixture was first used in armies to frighten and kill enemies. Later, it was used to mark celebrations in European courts.

To put on a display of pyrotechnics (the official term for fireworks), a firework engineer uses different fuses. The main fuse, which is filled with gunpowder, sets off the smaller fuses, which contain metal granules mixed with explosives.

The small fuses contain a time delay that, once ignited, shoot little colored stars into the sky!

A variety of chemical compounds can be added to the gunpowder to create colors, such as blue, yellow, and gold. To obtain blue, copper must be added; to obtain yellow, sodium is mixed in; and to attain a golden hue, iron. But in what proportions? Even today, firework engineers fiercely guard their secrets!

How do people live in prison?

When a person is convicted of having committed a major crime, there is usually no more appropriate a punishment than taking away his or her freedom. Even though it's normal to penalize criminal offenders, spending a lifetime behind bars is no picnic!

Imprisonment means being separated from your family and friends, lacking any kind of privacy, and having your mail read by others for reasons of security, to name just a few.

In prison, each day is identical: breakfast is served at 7:00 A.M., dinner is served at 6:00 P.M. . . . all under the watchful eyes of the guards.

Hours blend into one another, and it's easy to lose track of time. Days are spent doing repetitive activities: visits, walks in an enclosed space, a bit of physical activity, a visit to the library, reading or writing letters, and, for some, working in a workshop.

What day is it?

Even though prisoners can earn a bit of money through paid labor to enrich their daily lives (by renting a television, for example, or decorating the walls of their cell), they still live with the bare minimum compared to those in the free world.

27

How can I convince my mother that video games won't make me stupid?

This can be a fairly arduous task, considering that the vast majority of parents don't know the slightest thing about video games! And, in fact, seeing a child entirely consumed by the actions of a violent hero won't necessarily put a parent at ease, especially if the child explodes with rage in front of the television, clutching the controls like a lunatic! So it's up to you to prove the educational value of video games to skeptical adults.

Why not start by simply showing them your favorite game? Explain the rules and introduce the characters and the powers they have at their disposal . . . basically, describe why you find this particular game so intriguing!

However, beware of going too far. Your parents aren't fools. They'll see right through any attempt to exaggerate the benefits of video games! Remember to listen to their arguments, and negotiate specific times during which video-game playing will be allowed.

Excess of any kind is bad. In this case, staring at a screen for hours on end can have a hypnotic effect: you may become completely oblivious to your surroundings and find it hard to wake up to reality.

Why not ask one of your parents to play a game with you? You never know . . . with a bit of patience and indulgence, you may have found yourself a decent opponent!

28

How are babies made?

Adults sometimes don't like having to answer this question. They think it isn't appropriate for children, since it deals with sexual relations between a man and a woman.

From a purely biological standpoint, two specific cells must come together to make a baby: the male cell, called spermatozoa, which is produced in the father's genitalia, and the female cell, the ovum, or egg, which is in the mother.

Oh no, not the stork again!

I get no respect.

Perhaps we should rephrase our question and ask "How is life created?" or "How is life passed down to the next generation?" After all, expanding our vocabulary always gives us a greater appreciation for life.

As a result, all kinds of crazy stories have been told about where babies come from. Either a stork brings it home, or it was found in a cabbage patch or rosebushes. But if you ever stop to think about it, what is more natural than the birth of a child?

A natural pathway was designed in the woman's body for the father's sperm to reach the mother's ovum. The fusion of the two cells forms a tiny embryo, which develops over the course of nine months and is delivered as a baby.

But the birth of a child involves a lot more than just biology. "Making" a baby has a lot to do with chance, because one sperm among millions must join with the ovum to create an embryo. And choosing to make a baby in the first place depends on a man and a woman making a joint decision to create a new life.

How do we know what the future will hold?

For millennia, humans have wondered what life had in store for them: luck or misfortune? They wanted to know what lay before them in order to change their destiny, or succumb to it. What waited for them around the corner? Sickness? Love? Death?

Throughout the world, people have questioned the stars, precious stones, and even seashells to uncover clues about their future. In China, over 4,000 years ago, soothsayers used the shape of, and patterns on, a turtle's shell to predict their emperor's future. All in all, these methods have proven useless in attempting to shed light on human destiny.

I see, I see, I see . . .

that it's time to get my eyes checked!

Is it easier to predict the future of a planet? For example, figuring out how it will look several hundred years from now? A umber of scientists are trying o determine the future of the earth based on present-day observations. They take into ccount climate change, global warming, desert formation, deforestation, earthquakes, etc. . . .

But even in these cases, their predictions are based on working hypotheses regarding the evolution of our planet. No one can say with any degree of certainty what the earth will be like tomorrow, even if it depends a great deal on how we treat it today! No matter what, it's impossible to know what the future holds!

How do plants grow in the desert?

The plants that we see in the desert are true heroes! To grow, they have to fight against dryness, withstand extremely high daytime temperatures and cold nighttime temperatures, and make do with soil rich in salt and low in fertilizer.

Three main types of plants have adapted to these conditions, each in its own way: annuals, phreatophytes, and xerophytes. Annuals are very patient: their seeds can survive for three years without water and still bloom. It's easy to see why they're called "dormant." Annuals spring to life for a period of only a few weeks, and only during one season.

Phreatophytes grow a network of long underground roots from which new ones sprout. As they are deeply entrenched in the ground, they are able to resist extreme heat as well as sandstorms. They flower every other year.

Xerophytes are known for their extreme resistance to drought. These plants absorb and store even the tiniest drops of water. A cactus is perhaps the most well-known member of this group. After a rain shower in the desert, a big cactus can absorb many liters of water, and stock a reserve for the dry months that lay ahead. Now that's heroic!

How do artists see the world?

Sometimes, when we look at portraits painted by Picasso, Chagall, or Duchamp, or landscapes painted by Matisse or van Gogh, we may wonder if these painters had problems with their vision! Have you ever seen a triangle-shaped nose, a head bigger than its body, or purple trees?

But painters don't wear special glasses! Art isn't a question of sight but of observation and interpretation. Even if two painters went to the same art school, had the same teachers, spent the same number of hours working on their techniques, and used the same props or models, their paintings still wouldn't look alike.

Hello, Mr. Picasso. How do you do?

See for yourself by doing this experiment with your brothers and sisters: Take a piece of paper and crayons and draw a picture of your family. Now compare your results. You'll notice that the difference between your drawing and those of your brothers and sisters is the result of the unique way in which you see your family. Maybe you've sketched yourself taller than everyone, or your younger sister may have placed herself in the middle of her drawing, and didn't include you!

Each human being is unique, and the same goes for the way he or she sees the world. One person's sense of reality is very different from another's, and can't be reproduced.

The same thing goes for painters. Rather than try to capture reality on a canvas, they paints their ideas and perceptions of people and the world.

33

How do you succeed in life?

Your teachers and parents may have given you the impression that getting good grades is the key to a successful life. By that logic, the best student in class would be the most successful later on in life.

However, even if knowledge and competence can help you land a job and achieve a certain level of success, they aren't the sole prerequisites of being successful!

Fortunately, a successful life is not measured by how many diplomas you receive, nor by the profession you choose, and least of all by the amount of money you have in your bank account. Success can't be planned far in advance. There isn't a single pathway leading toward fame and fortune.

So what does it mean to have a successful life? It's a personal feeling more than anything else: living a life that includes everything you always hoped for. A successful life incorporates everything: our relationships with other people and our experiences, our knowledge and convictions, as well as the mistakes, doubts, and failures that make us human.

It takes time to succeed in life. Gandhi, the spiritual and political leader of India, fought against racism, religious discrimination, and violence until his death. For him, success in life meant fighting until the end.

How can a child live with only one parent?

One parent . . .

is largely sufficient!

Our birth required the joint participation of a man and a woman, our biological parents. Our continued growth and development requires, more than anything else, a stable and loving environment, be it in the presence of one parent or both, or our adoptive parents.

Each family is unique. That's why it's so hard to come up with a general answer to a question that differs according to who is being asked. When you live with only one parent, it may sometime signal that your family has overcome turbulent past. But it doesn't mean that you have to live on your own, completely cut off from the outside world.

Sometimes children find role models outside of their immediate family, seeking guidance from other family members, teachers, or friends.

The difficulty of being the child of a single parent can be having to take on the role of "little husband" or "little wife." Sometimes, single parents put too much pressure on their children to take on responsibility and deal with family problems.

But children should have only one role in the lives of their parents: their own, that of children who need security, love, recreation, education and a social life. They should never have to fill a hole in the lives of their parents. Remember, as hard as it is for children to say no to their moms or dads, it's more important for them to have a healthy childhood.

How do you get ideas?

It's hard to say exactly how ideas form in our brains, or how we use them to express ourselves coherently.

A lot has been said about the origin of ideas. Are we born with a neat little suitcase of ideas that we can search through to figure out how best to structure our comprehension of the world?

Or do ideas come from what we see, hear, taste, feel, and touch, combined in new ways?

Actually, our senses help us to be imaginative, inventive, and creative, and to generate new ideas. But we use our reasoning to arrange our perceptions of the world.

Being curious, observing the world around us (for example, nature), reading, debating, traveling, meeting new people, and discovering works of arts—this is what inspires new ideas.

Therefore, the more you ask questions and challenge yourself to find answers to them on your own, the more ideas you'll have. And the more ideas you have, the more chances you'll have to think of something great!

How do whales sing?

As for many animals, the language whales use to communicate with one another is made up of codes and signals: wags of the tail or fins, acrobatic movements under the water, noisy dives, and calls and whistles.

Even though both males and females are capable of producing sounds to communicate, only the male whales sing—during the mating season (in order to attract the females) and during the winter migration.

Some whales can sing for over fifteen minutes without taking a breath. Oh, the things we do for love! Females can hear these declarations of love from miles away, thanks to sound waves emitted by these calls, which travel through the water.

Bravo!

Each year, at the end of the mating season, male whales may learn a new song from the other whales, and add it to their song repertory. Every five years or so, their melodies change completely.

Singing whales don't tire easily: their concerts can last for hours, even days, on end. This way they can attract even the most stubborn females!

How can God hear us?

Does God have big ears, like antennae, that can hear the messages we send? No matter which religion you belong to, picturing God has always been a challenge.

Humans have long created God in their own image. They gave God a face, a human body, and feelings—a visible image to behold during prayer.

But if humans can talk to God, how does God hear them? For those who believe in God, the word "hear," which also means "listen" and "understand," shows that God is not indifferent to them. God is ever-present, though invisible.

Believers feel that God is close to them and brings meaning to their lives. It is this particular relationship between humans and God that is so special, and so vital.

How are tunnels built underwater?

With a pick and a shovel? Sure, but that might take a while! Digging a tunnel underwater follows the same principle as drilling a tunnel through a mountain, except you have to dig very deep to get under the marine floor.

Digging underneath the earth's surface requires a kind of giant mechanical mole: a tunnel-boring machine. This is a giant cylinder, set up on tracks, whose rotating head is so powerful it can pound through even the toughest rock. The conveyor belts to either side of the cylinder function as arms that clear away loose material from the excavated earth. The rock face is covered in either concrete or metal to stabilize the tunnel walls and avoid collapse.

A tunnel-boring machine can dig more than two hundred feet per day. That's a lot! But a mole, which weighs a mere five ounces, can dig up to sixty feet a day! Given its small stature, that's quite an accomplishment!

One of the longest underground tunnels in the world today is the Eurotunnel, which links France and Great Britain through the English Channel. It measures just over thirty miles in length and can be crossed by train in just twenty minutes at speeds of up to a hundred miles an hour.

How were colors made before paint tubes existed?

According to some estimates, humans began to draw as far back as 40,000 years ago, even though they started to write only 3,000 years ago! Drawing and painting played an integral role in people's need to express themselves and their desire to understand the world around them.

In the Stone Age, humans already knew how clay, ashes from bones, and vegetal pigments could be mixed with water or grease to obtain paints suitable for drawing on rock faces or cave walls. The beauty of these drawings is still awe-inspiring today, in every part of the world.

Where would I be without my paint set . . .

Throughout history, various civilizations searched for colors vibrant enough to pay homage to the beauty of their god or gods. They dug through the soil to obtain browns, reds, and yellows; minerals gave them greens and blues; chalk and clay produced whites; even seashells yielded colors such as crimson.

Much like chefs, painters have their own recipes for enhancing their colors and diversifying their palettes. The precious powders obtained from the earth's soil can be used as they are, or heated and mixed with water, egg whites, or oils.

Even though some painters prefer to use these ancient techniques to derive their paints, the development of more industrial techniques has led to the production of paints in every shade of the rainbow. But don't let that stop you from experimenting to create your own unique colors!

42

How does a person become crazy?

The words "crazy" and "insane" are used in our daily vocabulary to describe everything that falls outside the realm of sensible and normal. But specialists see insanity as something far more serious: it starts when a person finds it increasingly difficult to live in society because he or she feels, either consciously or subconsciously, that he or she no longer belongs in it.

The biological factor: Our brain is an extremely complex organ charged with the task of processing all kinds of information, thanks to an elaborate network of connected cells. Sometimes, however, without explanation, certain cells can't connect, or become disconnected, resulting in abnormal or dangerous behavior toward oneself or others.

Insanity isn't a sickness that we can catch, like a cold. Rather, it's a troubling mental condition caused by a number of different factors.

I'm crazy about you, doctor!

A person may also become more withdrawn, due to negative influences stemming from his or her social or familial environment. In this case, the illness is caused by psychological factors.

Many such illnesses, such as depression, schizophrenia, or psychosis, have been diagnosed in varying degrees of severity. Some can be treated successfully, others cannot. But medication and other forms of treatment have been used by doctors and therapists to ease a patient's suffering.

Craziness and insanity aren't labels under which all kinds of abnormal behavior should be categorized. Remember, there's a big difference between eccentricity and illness!

43

How can I satisfy my **curiosity?**

You might think of curiosity as a flaw, especially if you find yourself tearing through someone else's belongings or peering through a keyhole. Sometimes, yes. But without curiosity, we might not even be here!

Potatoes were discovered by digging through the ground, the magnifying glass and microscope were invented in order to see the tiniest known particles, and rockets were designed to allow us to bring back parts of the moon. Since the beginning of time, people have always looked beyond what's right in front of them, to discover new lands or to better understand their environment.

People created the notions of gods and spirits to explain death, illness, and meteorological phenomena, by using their fertile imaginations. But some people weren't satisfied and came up with their own theoretical explanations.

Discovery often arises as a result of dissatisfaction. In questioning established beliefs, we create an opportunity for new explanations.

To prove that there is reason to doubt something, you must first come up with an alternative theory and put it through a number of tests until it becomes accepted as the new rule, susceptible to its own scrutiny in the future. In the past, death was thought to be caused by an evil spirit. And the earth was once thought to be flat . . .

Great discoveries always shock the established order of the day, and history is full of explorers and inventors who were scorned during their lifetime. And yet, we are where we are today thanks to them and their many trials and errors.

How is striped toothpaste made?

Whether they're red, green, or blue, toothpaste stripes have no apparent function other than to make the toothpaste look prettier in order to persuade consumers to buy one brand over another, depending on their taste and color preferences. But regardless of how they look, how did the stripes get in the tube in the first place?

There's no magic in toothpaste stripes, only one thing to keep in mind: the nozzle of a toothpaste tube is fitted with a special device, less than a centimeter in length and pierced with a ring of small holes. Unlike a normal tube filled end to end with white paste, striped toothpaste contains two other compartments on each side filled with colored paste.

When the tube is squeezed, the white paste pushes on the compartments of colored paste, which in turn pushes through the holes in the tube's nozzle. The pastes come out together in stripes.

The mystery is solved! To better understand the mechanics of how it works, ask a grown-up to cut a toothpaste tube in half, lengthwise, and see for yourself!

How was the earth discovered to be round?

I know it seems strange...

but you'll have to get used to it!

A disk floating on the sea, an egg, a pear, a pinecone, or a rounded cylinder: almost all of these descriptions have been used at one time or another to describe the shape of the earth before it had been entirely explored.

In the days of Greek antiquity, wise men claimed that the earth was round, but no one believed them. However, they noticed that when traveling from north to south, the star constellations usually visible in the sky would disappear, and others would appear in their place.

Much later, an expedition sailed off to circumnavigate the globe. The voyage of Ferdinand Magellan, which left Spain on September 20, 1519, cleared up any remaining doubts: his ships traveled from west to east and arrived at the same spot three years later, without ever turning around.

Magellan and his crew thus made the first tour of the world, proving once and for all that the earth is round. Before their trip, not everyone agreed about the earth's shape. Humanity saw itself as the center of the universe, so the earth was thought to be a flat plate surrounded by ocean! Then again, without any form of verification, everything seems possible!

How can we be sure we've found **true love?**

Your heart beats faster when you hear his voice. You blush when he looks at you. You stutter and stumble over your words, even though you had a whole speech prepared . . . It's pretty clear from these scenarios that love has taken hold of you. But how can you be sure that it's true love, love with a capital L, the kind that lasts a lifetime?

Lust and love are two very different emotions. Lust is linked to immediate desires and pleasure. You may hardly know a person, and yet she has cast a spell over you, inspiring a kind of giddy excitement. You find yourself dreaming of your love, or imagining her in different situations. In fact, you project your own desires onto her, without taking into account her own.

Being in love is a different story. Love takes time to grow and requires that two people truly know each other. The dreaminess is still there, but it's a dream shared by two people who walk along the same path, hand in hand. You love and are loved in return, and find it difficult to imagine life without the other.

But whether you are in lust or love, there's no guarantee that the other person feels the same way. And so? Well, what's nice about love is that, in the end, you can never be sure about anything. That's why it's so important to be careful, don't jump into anything too fast, and always be in touch with your inner feelings.

Uh, I hope it's not contagious.

Bua, bua, bua.

How were museums invented?

Humans have long had a tendency to collect souvenirs. Children pile their treasures in boxes hidden under their beds. Adults accumulate belongings. Countries build museums.

Prehistoric caves that contained sculpted bones, pebbles, and seashells have been discovered. Egyptians accumulated all kinds of precious objects as a way of embellishing the afterlife.

From antiquity through the Middle Ages, leaders and religious figures from different civilizations assembled a large number of works of art in their palaces and churches for the benefit of the public.

Starting in the sixteenth century, aristocratic Italian families set an example for all the other European courts by assembling collections of rare objects, thereby initiating the artistic movements of their time. But these were not yet museums, only private collections.

Little by little, these rare objects and works of art began to be classified by genre and date, and were dedicated to the halls of the great palaces, called "galleries." Artists and students were invited to come and admire them. During the French Revolution, these buildings and collections were nationalized and displayed to the general public. And the first museums were born.

How was it decided that a **week** would consist of seven days?

To better organize life in society, humans had to find a way to structure their time according to their work schedule or seasonal changes. Thanks to their keen sense of observation, the calendar was invented.

The moon orbits the earth about once every twenty-eight days, and goes through various phases: new moon, first quarter, full moon, and third quarter. When you divide these twenty-eight days by these four phases, you get a period of seven days: one week.

The Chaldeans of Babylonia were the first to perform this division, in around 500 B.C., and adapt it to their daily lives.

After them, the Hebrews gave the week religious significance by drawing on the Bible, which says that God created the world in six days, and rested on the seventh. This seventh day corresponds to the Sabbath in Jewish tradition.

But it was in Rome, under the emperor Augustus, that the week as we know it today was definitively adopted. Each day (or "diem" in Latin) was correlated to a different planet and named after it.

In English, we have three days that still correspond to the Roman gods: the Moon (Monday), Saturn (Saturday), and the Sun (Sunday).

How is justice fair?

"Justice" refers to the principle of equality between individuals. As an institution, justice mediates conflicts between individuals and permits each individual to exercise his or her rights. But is justice influenced by the victims of crimes, by what is written in the media, or by the opinions of others? Is there a type of justice that applies solely to the rich, and another to the poor? In other words, is justice truly just?

Justice is an institution administered by the state, but judges don't depend on it for their ruling. They judge by way of their soul and their conscience by looking at all the facts presented and the responsibility and actions of those accused. They never give in to pressure. And the government cannot influence their decisions.

If judges make mistakes, then "judicial errors" can be recognized, but this is very rare. We should have faith in the system of justice, which exists to protect the fundamental rights of each person: the right to life, liberty, and the pursuit of happiness; the right to leave your country and return to it; the right to practice your religion; the right to speak your mind; and the right to information . . .

In dictatorships, where the government controls everything, justice is no longer independent, but rather directed by the arbitrary authority of its rulers. Rather than guaranteeing rights, this system of justice denies fundamental rights to its citizens.

How can I explain to my family that my room is private?

"Do not enter!" The sign is written clearly on the door! But there's nothing you can do to enforce it. It's hard to create your own little space, where shoes, apple cores, empty soda cans, photos, books, discs, and secret drawers all coexist happily, in a state of complete disorder.

For millennia, humans have created boundaries between their world and the exterior world, between inside and out, public and private. There are rules in all societies governing when you can enter certain places and when you can't. The need to call your room your own—a small enclosed private space—is constant throughout time.

Although people in the West seek privacy, that may not always hold true for people in other societies, in which family members of all ages can live together in the same room. Private space is relative depending on culture. But it's fair to say that at one time or another, each person seeks a little peace and quiet.

You want your family to respect the privacy of your room because you consider it your little corner of freedom—an escape from communal living. And why not? Nobody ought to go into your closet, drawers, or other hidden places when you're not there.

It all comes down to trust between parents and children, brothers and sisters. But don't forget about reciprocity: other people's bedrooms are also private!

How do birds see us from high up in the sky?

They see us as big, dangerous, unappetizing, two-footed beasts! But seriously, from up high, birds see us just as clearly as though they were looking at us through binoculars.

Birds don't have trouble with their vision, even when they're flying high up in the sky. They have more visual cells per square millimeter than humans do, so they see eight times better than we do. Some species have a perfect 360-degree field of vision!

Like us, birds can distinguish colors, but they appear far more vivid to them because they can see ultraviolet, whereas we can't.

Birds have lots of skills that people value. In addition to flying, birds have a better sense of direction than we do, and faster instincts when facing danger (obstacles or predators).

How can we be certain that we're not living in a dream?

Is our life nothing but a dream—an illusion? What if we were like Alice in Wonderland or Pinocchio or imaginary characters straight out of fairy tales and other stories? We might think we were real, but we would actually be living in a world of fiction.

When we're asleep, we can't always tell the difference between dreams and reality. The people we see, the adventures we embark on, and the emotions we feel when we're dreaming may seem very real.

A long time ago, a Chinese sage by the name of Chuang Tzu said: "I dreamed that I was a butterfly, and when I woke up I wondered whether I was a man who dreamed he was a butterfly, or a butterfly dreaming he was a man." Is it that easy to confuse dreams and reality?

As we grow and our brains continue to develop, we learn to distinguish dreams from reality. Once we become adults, we see things a lot more clearly, and there's not a lot of room for confusion.

Everyone creates his or her own little world in dreams, kind of like a film set, that differs from one person to another. In the real world, on the other hand, everyone perceives the same things—the same landscape, the same city—and this general perception never changes. Whatever dreams may come to us at night, we know that once we open our eyes, the world will be as it was when we first closed them . . .

How do fish sleep?

How do fish sleep when they get tired of swimming? Under a bedspread or down comforter? On a bed of algae? Inside a shell?

Do fish actually sleep or are they only pretending to? They never seem to tire of staring at us with their big eyes. And for good reason! Fish don't have eyelids. A transparent membrane covers their eyes, like a pair of tiny scuba-diving goggles!

So if you happen to see a fish perfectly still, almost immobile, lulled by the gentleness of the river's current, chances are it's taking a short rest. Try not to disturb it!

How can I say what I feel?

There are times when you don't want to join a discussion in progress for fear of others' judgments and opinions. You might be afraid to say something stupid or stumble over your words, so you choose to say nothing, thereby giving the illusion of indifference.

But why keep quiet when you don't agree with something? Though you may run the risk of being judged, talked back to, or even insulted, it is still important to speak your mind and stick up for what you believe in. This is what healthy debate is all about.

A good way to overcome your fear of speaking is to clarify your ideas in your mind first, before you begin to speak. Remembering to take deep breaths is also important when you want to express your opinions calmly, without aggression, and defend them using two or three simple arguments.

But be careful! Words can be a formidable weapon, so you'll want to think before you speak and measure the consequences of your words, so as not to offend or humiliate anyone. Saying exactly what you feel is not an invitation to harm others, but to respect them.

Avoid long-winded monologues, loud interruptions, or slamming doors. After all, you aren't acting in a play, and these antics won't make you popular with your listeners. You must learn to accept others' opinions and criticism, but not at the cost of abandoning your own position.

How was music invented?

To explain how music came about, a number of legends claim that the gods were the musicians of their time: in Greece, Apollo played the lyre; in India, the god Sri Krishna preferred the flute . . . These divine beings were generous with their art, but for good reason: they taught men how to play instruments, so they, in turn, could play for them.

Others believe that music, as indicated by its name, was a gift from the muses. They say that these Greek goddesses turned music, poetry, and dance into an art form so we could sing their praises and give them cult status. Sacred music linked the world of the gods with that of the mortals.

Legends aside, prehistoric people understood early on that tapping on a shell, pebble, bamboo branch, or taut animal fur produced very different sounds. The pleasure they derived from this experiment, coupled with the effect of the produced sounds, made it tempting to repeat and continually harmonize them.

BONG!

Good!

Much time passed before instruments capable of reproducing the sounds of the wind, water, and birdcalls were created. The Egyptian harp, for example, is only about 5,000 years old.

How can I be accepted into a group?

Being part of a group brings about feelings of security and recognition, but it might foster dependency, uniformity, and a loss of freedom. In fact, groups have the unfortunate tendency of being exclusive and therefore intolerant of difference, change, and the unknown.

Wanting at all costs to be integrated into a certain group is not a trivial matter: before you jump in, it's best to inquire about the mentality of the group and understand your motivation for wanting to join it.

Joining a group requires that you prove yourself, and your intentions, to the members. This may not be such a simple task. Your fear of being judged, and the ensuing lack of self-confidence under the circumstances, may mask your true personality and give a bad impression.

The most agreeable groups are often those that are the most open-minded, for example teams that revolve around sports, games, or art. A strong team is one that sets out to achieve a common goal, with each of its members contributing in a significant way.

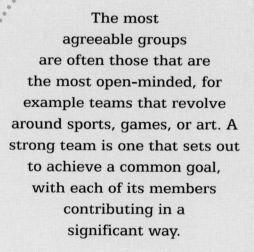

So try your best to overcome your shyness and prove your value and self-worth to others. Despite your best intentions, the group may still deny you access either because there's no space left or because they simply fear what they don't know. But don't let that get you down! After all, there's nothing preventing you from going out and starting your own group!

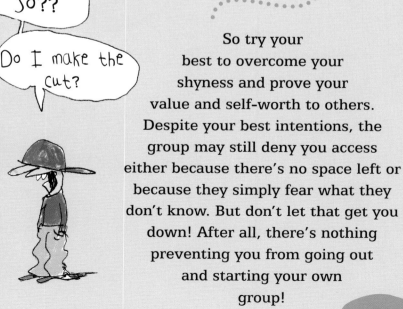

How can a person live without love?

Some parents can't—or don't know how to—properly love their child, so much so that the child may go through life feeling unloved. This kind of treatment can cause serious injury to the child, and prevent him or her from growing up with a sense of security.

Childish fears, adolescent rebellion, and adult anguish—all these forms of human distress have one thing in common: a feeling of abandonment caused by a lack of love.

But what's the point of growing up when nobody respects or cares for you? Unloved children may never develop confidence in themselves or others, and could spend the rest of their lives yearning for love.

Sometimes, however, people can develop the patience, affection, and tenderness to make up for their loveless childhoods. They may start to believe in others, because others took the time to believe in them.

But whether you're a child or an adult, it's impossible to live without love. Love gives us an identity, makes us feel respected, and enriches our lives.

How were national flags invented?

Regardless of their shape or color, flags once served as the civil or military emblems of a tribe, lord, family, or entire city. They functioned as a kind of "business card," signaling to visitors exactly who ruled there.

In the past, flags were used to announce a state of quarantine (for example, when a city was in the throes of an epidemic). In the nautical world, colored flags hoisted on masts allowed boats to communicate with one another over long distances. Warning flags went up immediately if pirate ships were known to be in the vicinity!

When countries were founded, flags were transformed into national flags. Every nation in the world is identified by its own unique flag. The colors and the references incorporated on them are symbols dating from a country's history.

Hmmm... I think we should go with this one.

For example, the colors of the American flag are red, white, and blue. The thirteen stripes represent the thirteen original colonies, and the fifty stars represent each of the fifty United States.

How do **children** train to become soldiers?

War has killed nearly two million children since 1990, destroyed schools, and wiped out entire villages. Six million children have been injured, and at least a million orphaned.

Today, 300,000 child soldiers fight in armed conflicts in more than thirty conflicts around the world. These statistics—made public by UNICEF in December 2004—are staggering.

The majority of child soldiers are drugged to numb them to fear and violence. Whether they live in Burma, Africa, the Philippines, Latin America, or Sri Lanka, child soldiers are usually recruited by rebel groups fighting against the government. They fight on war's front lines, machine guns in hand. Some are as young as eight years old.

In Africa, for example, some Rwandan children, recruited and pressured by commandos, were forced to commit atrocities against people in their own village. Though girls sometimes participate in armed conflict, often they are sexually abused by the adult soldiers.

Left on their own, without their families, homes, or education, and without a moral compass teaching them right from wrong, these children have their childhoods irremediably shattered.

A number of child protection organizations have called upon the United Nations to punish countries that enlist soldiers under the age of eighteen for crimes against humanity.

How do blind people read?

Blind people read with their hands. In 1821, Louis Braille, who lost his sight at the age of three, learned about a system called "night writing" used by the army in the beginning of the nineteenth century. This system enabled soldiers to read and share secret messages in the dark, without being seen by the enemy. Braille realized that this system could be adapted for use by the blind.

I have eyes on the tips of my fingers.

The Braille system is made up of sixty-four combinations of raised dots made by a special pen or typewriter. These combinations cover every letter of the alphabet, punctuation marks, numbers, mathematical signs, and even musical notes.

To read, you touch the raised type with your fingertips, from left to right, just like regular reading. Braille is a complete reading and writing system using six dots in different positions in a rectangular cell (a maximum of two dots from top to bottom and three across).

Braille has been adapted to almost every language, including Chinese. But many texts have yet to be transcribed into Braille. Greater progress is needed so that the blind have just as much access to great works of literature as the seeing.

For example, the letter "A" is symbolized by a dot in the upper left-hand corner of the rectangular cell. To obtain the letter "B," a second dot is added underneath the one written for "A."

How do roosters know when to crow?

A rooster crows as soon as he wakes up to impress the chickens in the poultry yard. But little does he know that he performs the function of an alarm clock for the people around him!

Before the invention of the lightbulb, farms operated according to the rhythm of the days. People, like animals, organized their days around sunlight: they woke up and went to bed at the same time as the sun.

As soon as his eyes open, the rooster takes his place on the roof of the chicken coop and crows to whoever will listen that he is the best and most beautiful of them all. And woe to he who attempts to step into his territory! For the most part, the rooster wakes at dawn. Therefore, the rooster's crow announces to all that it's time to wake up.

Unfortunately, sometimes a loud noise or a bout of insomnia might awaken the rooster prematurely, prompting him to crow in the middle of the night! Farmers, exhausted by these untimely wake-ups, have learned to rely on their alarm clocks for their wake-up call, rather than trust these self-appointed "rulers" of the chicken coop.

How do you ask for forgiveness?

Crash! The baseball shatters the neighbor's window! Yikes! After a stupid stunt like that, you may feel like running away, becoming invisible, or, worse, blaming it on another person. "I didn't do it! He did it . . ."

Nobody's perfect! Clumsiness is excusable, and it's always best to try to repair the damage. On the other hand, when you deliberately blame another person for your own mistake, it's no longer a stupid stunt— it's an injustice. How can you ask for forgiveness from someone you've wrongly accused? That can be awkward! It's not easy to admit making a mistake. You'll probably hear lots of bad excuses before a person can admit that he or she has hurt someone else.

But making amends to those you've betrayed is the only way to regain their trust. The words and actions you use to excuse yourself should be accompanied by a promise that you won't repeat the same mistake!

Asking for forgiveness requires courage and sincerity. It's always best to use simple words and affectionate gestures to renew ties with those you've hurt, rather than a long, drawn-out apology. What's essential is that you feel responsible for your acts and prove your good faith in order to regain their trust.

How can we know what awaits us after we die?

For millennia, people have feared the unknown. As a result, they try to explain what they don't understand, such as the passage between life and death.

They've wondered about the survival of the soul: Does the soul live on after the body decomposes? Do the dead embark on a whole new life? Can they communicate with us? Do they have any influence over the world of the living?

Many people thought that the dead went to either heaven or hell. They thought of life as continuing into the afterworld, and that the dead could make contact with the living.

According to traditional African beliefs, the dead live side by side with the living. They see us, protect us, and can seek revenge upon us if we forget them. Hindus believe in reincarnation, the idea that the dead come back to life as another human, animal, or vegetal form until they attain perfection.

Many faiths— Buddhism, Judaism, Christianity, Islam, and Hinduism— believe that life doesn't end at death. Death is viewed as a necessary pathway to a new life, one that is better and closer to God. But, alas, these are only beliefs, not certainties.

How can we avoid going to school?

School is mandatory until the age of sixteen, so you have no choice but to attend. Even if you complain of a stomachache the day of a big exam, there's no avoiding the fact that at one time or another, you have to go back to class!

Sprinting to school in the mornings out of excitement to learn new things isn't exactly normal, but neither is hating it to the point where you refuse to set foot in the classroom. Disliking school that much is the result of deeper reasons: the fear of failure or ranking last in the class, the fear of getting picked on or insulted if you don't understand a certain exercise, even the fear of verbal attack.

The first known systems of education date from about 4000 B.C. Obviously, humanity's need to educate itself didn't start yesterday! In the United States, school became mandatory around the turn of the twentieth century, giving each person the right to an education, no matter what socioeconomic class he or she belonged to.

Free, secular, public schools can't impose any specific mode of thinking on the student body. These schools teach the basics of communication, thought, and reflection.

Whatever the reason, a solution must be found to remedy the situation. Cutting class isn't the answer! If your fear of school is so strong that you wish to avoid it altogether, talk about it with your parents or a trustworthy teacher. They're there to lend a helping hand.

How do glowworms light up?

Humans have long depended on artificial light to find their way in the dark. At first they used fire, then, eventually, electricity. But when it comes to lighting, there is one bug with far more expertise than us: glowworms.

The glowworm belongs to the firefly family, which possesses special light organs located on the underside of the abdomen.

At certain times of the night, particularly during the mating period in the summertime, the glowworm emits an enzyme called "luciferase" that, when combined with oxygen, generates light. The female glowworm signals her presence to the male by flickering her light. This way, the couple can find each other in the dark.

Look out, dear! I'm lighting up!

In South Asia, some species of fireflies meet in trees by the thousands and flash on and off, all night long . . .

How do you make friends?

A new school, new neighborhood, new state . . . one day you may find yourself in a completely new world where nobody knows you, and you may begin to feel very alone. Though your parents may tell you that it's only temporary, the prospect of not having any friends can be terrifying.

Then again, how many times a day do you greet a stranger with a simple "Hello"? More often than you realize. This greeting—this first casual "Hello"—opens the door to getting to know someone better.

But a simple "How are you?" is not enough. To make a friend, you have to develop certain ties with that person. This requires time and effort. Having a friend means having responsibility. So is there some kind of magic recipe for making friends?

Greeting someone has always been, in every culture, a sign of peace. Even a long time ago, a courteous greeting proved that one came as a friend, not an enemy.

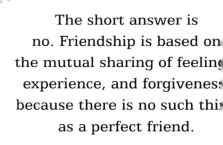

The short answer is no. Friendship is based on the mutual sharing of feeling, experience, and forgiveness, because there is no such thing as a perfect friend.

The great writer Montaigne, when asked how he chose his friends, replied, "Because I'm me and he's he . . ." That's a pretty good way of summarizing the mystery of friendship, don't you think?

How does a veterinarian know **where** an **animal hurts?**

Aside from in fairy tales, lions and sheep don't talk, and they certainly don't complain of sinus problems or sore throats! Does this mean that veterinarians are fluent in the language that animals use to communicate?

Not really. But their many years of schooling helped them develop expertise in how animals function. And they've also learned a thing or two about the various illnesses that can afflict them.

When the problem is obvious— such as when an animal gets a pebble stuck in its paw, making it limp—the diagnosis is easy to make. But sometimes the cause of an animal's ailment is more complex, and a more thorough examination is required.

In this case, the veterinarian might ask the owner questions about the animal's habits, and whether there have been any changes in the animal's behavior. Has it lost its appetite recently? Does it seem agitated? Aggressive? Or does it seem more withdrawn?

The answers to these questions give the veterinarian clues as to what the animal's symptoms might be. Veterinarians also rely on specialized instruments and imaging—such as X-rays and ultrasounds—which help them figure out what's ailing an animal beyond simple appearances.

Ahhhhh!

Say Ahhhhh!

71

How can I **resist** a chocolate doughnut?

Having a sweet tooth isn't a problem, unless it starts to affect your weight and health. One of the most difficult things is learning how to resist excess: excess cake, candy, and other sweets. Otherwise, you'll end up with indigestion! Just as the wise ancient Greeks used to say: the right amount is that which everyone agrees on. No more, no less.

To avoid a chocolate doughnut, all you have to do is steer clear of donut shops along your path, either by turning around or quickly crossing the street when you see one. Or try to resist the temptation by taking deep breaths, or thinking of something else.

After all, why do we yearn to satisfy our cravings and gorge on sweets? Is it because we're that hungry, or do we simply want to fill the world with a bit of sweetness?

Doctors know that the sugar we ingest from sugar cubes, pastries, and starches acts as "fuel" for our brains.

When we're stressed, our brains requires sugar to calm down. And that explains our craving for sweets! So, if a harmless thing like a chocolate doughnut provides comfort, why should we resist it?

How do rainbows form?

A long time ago, a rainbow was thought to be a bridge linking earth and heaven, the home of the gods.

Nowadays, we know that a rainbow is a physical phenomenon that occurs when it's raining while the sun is shining.

At first glance, sunlight appears white. But in reality, the color white doesn't exist in nature! Sunlight is actually composed of different colors: red, orange, yellow, green, blue, indigo, and violet.

When a ray of sunlight shines through a raindrop, it is refracted, and the light splits into a multitude of colors.

Because the water droplets are round, they each project a circular halo of color, making the arched shape we know so well. The sunlight emerging from millions of raindrops creates a rainbow.

So are rainbows as round and circular as a drop of water? Well, yes, but from where we're standing, we can only see half of the circle. To see the rainbow in its entirety, you'd have to be in an airplane . . .

How do we evolve?

Evolution actually evolves—everything changes with time! Scientists have found that from Big Bang (the great cosmic explosion that gave rise to the universe, some ten or twenty billion years ago) through the emergence of human beings, evolution has become increasingly complex.

First there were the original particles of matter that made up the universe, followed by atoms and molecules—then the first live cells.

Evolution progressed from organisms made up of one cell (unicellular) to the appearance of human beings, organisms composed of billions of cells (multicellular), and possessing highly developed and complex brains.

But since the emergence of the Cro-Magnon man, who first appeared some 40,000 years ago, the human body has evolved little over the years. The morphology (or shape) of the human species has remained virtually unchanged.

From that moment on, human evolution was marked by the acquisition of skills and experience, which allowed human beings to perfect their knowledge in everything from the mastery of fire to the discovery of new planets. In addition to skills and knowledge, humans have also acquired freedom. We're willing to bet that humanity has plenty of good days ahead!

How can I tell my parents that I get scared when they yell at me?

Screaming at another person—whether it's justified or not—is an aggressive act that doesn't resolve anything. It doesn't make you right, and it doesn't lend you authority.

Parents sometimes yell at their children because they fear they might be endangered, or that they'll fail. Because they're already burdened with problems related to work, money, and health, parents remain on edge, and their anxiety manifests itself through screaming.

Once this stress is relieved, everything goes back to normal, like the calm after a big storm. But even if you understand the reasons for it, their outbreaks can still cause emotional pain.

No matter what their reasons are for yelling, it's important to tell your parents how you feel about it, so that it doesn't become a habit. They will take your request to heart.

However, if you can't get through to them, and if their yelling bothers you to such a point that it becomes a form of daily abuse, don't hesitate to seek help outside your family!

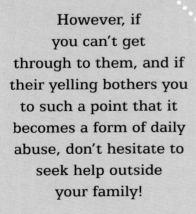

How can we help the poor?

You tell yourself that it's impossible to ignore the tragedies of the world—or even of your own community or neighborhood. Sometimes you feel the urge to roll up your sleeves and do something rather than turn a blind eye to other people's problems.

But you may not always know how to help people without hurting or judging them. It's not easy. In addition to the logistical problems of shelter, food, and work, hope is often what is most lacking in the lives of the poor.

The first step toward helping the poor live better lives is to change our perception of them. By doing so, you'll soon begin to think of spontaneous ways of helping them financially, and how to best go about it.

The most important thing to remember is to treat others the way you would like to be treated in return: with respect.

How do **broken bones** heal?

Our skeleton—the sturdy framework that holds us together and gets us around—consists of no fewer than 206 different bones. Whether they're short, long, or flat, our bones are covered by a bone tissue composed of the nutrients and minerals that makes them strong.

Throughout our lives, our bone tissue undergoes continual breakdown in order to release calcium into our bloodstream, and then the tissue rebuilds itself.

Sometimes, one or more of our bones may break due to a bad fall or an accident. By looking at an X-ray of the injured area, a doctor can determine the extent of the damage and how best to treat it. More often than not, the fracture will be clean. It will usually heal completely if it is kept in a cast or splint for several weeks.

But if the bone is displaced or chipped, plates and screws must be surgically implanted before it can be set in a cast.

Of course, it isn't the cast itself that heals the bone. The cast helps diminish the movement of the arm or leg, so it can heal faster. When the injury is immobilized, the process of bone-tissue restoration can begin. The new tissue is what seals the broken bone back together, like glue.

How can I **admit** that I don't like sports?

Many of the kids in your class wear football or baseball shirts emblazoned with the names and numbers of their favorite players. This conveys their love of the game and how, one day, they want to be the next sports superstar. Some other kids are obsessed with television shows, and some dream of becoming world-famous singers.

But what if neither of these things appeals to you? Does that mean there's something wrong with you? That you're abnormal? Crazy? Don't we maintain the right to our own tastes?

Of course! But you shouldn't go around criticizing others because they don't like the same things as you. Claiming your superiority over others and making fun of their tastes is tantamount to excluding them, and thereby excluding yourself.

It's important to be open-minded and tolerant of a wide range of tastes and opinions. But it's not always easy.

If you don't like the same things as others, try to tell them gently, without sarcasm, that you prefer other activities. You may even pique their interest in things *you* like to do!

That said, the fact that you don't share a passion for sports or music stardom with your friends doesn't mean that you don't have anything in common with them. There are still plenty of other things you agree on. Luckily, sharing interests isn't the only way of getting along with others!

How do migrating birds keep from getting lost?

Each spring, swallows start a new family. But did you know that they always return to the same nest they constructed the year before? Not their cousin's, or their neighbor's. Their own!

There are more than 9,000 known species of birds. Of these, about half migrate during the changing of seasons, to hunt for food. Obviously, this practice isn't new! As a result of numerous observations, scientists speculate that the origin of migration goes back to the Ice Age.

More than 15,000 years ago, most of the Northern Hemisphere was covered in a layer of ice, forcing all of its living beings southward. When the climate warmed up, birds retained the habit of migrating from north to south, and back again.

Scientists can't fully explain how migrating birds develop their sense of direction. However, it's possible that they use several different systems and types of information to orient themselves, together or separately: for example, the position of the sun in the sky, or the stars.

Birds also use their visual memory, which, like a camera, can capture the topography of the areas they travel through. They remember the shapes of the landscape—the hills, plains, and rivers. Their olfactory memory (the memory of odors) also helps them find their way around. Migratory birds make use of their internal compass to distinguish between variations in the earth's magnetic field.

The wheatear bird can cover more than 20,000 miles a year between Alaska and South Africa without getting lost. Despite all we know about migratory birds, this ability remains a mystery . . .

How can I tell on someone without being called a tattletale?

A bucket of water is strategically placed above the classroom door. The teacher opens the door, and splash! He ends up soaking wet! Furious, he demands that the culprit identify him- or herself, but the classroom remains silent. It's only a matter of time before he enforces a general punishment. What should you do?

If you are guilty of having committed this deplorable act, you should admit to it immediately, despite your fears, before others are wrongly accused. And if several of you pulled the stunt, you should convince all the others to turn themselves in to the teacher as well.

If you know who the perpetrators are and refuse to identify them, then you're as guilty as they are and should be punished equally. It's the same as if you were against the stunt from the start, and you were going to warn the teacher to go through a different door, but you were afraid to be taken for a tattletale!

Tattling shouldn't be done only to prevent danger or a serious crime. If you're a witness to, or victim of, a crime or violent act, then, by all means, don't hesitate to tell someone, such as your teacher.

But telling on someone so you come out looking good or blaming your own mistake on another person is disrespectful and simply wrong. Even if you're scared of being ridiculed, you should make a habit of thinking before you act, weigh the circumstances of telling on someone, and make the right decision.

Who did that?

He did it!

Who?

Um, I already told you.

How was medicine discovered?

Humans first discovered the benefits of herbs and plants in their environment by chance: cloves were discovered to be a good remedy for toothache, and poppy flowers were found to relive pain . . . Of course, there have also been some unfortunate accidents: the first person to have tasted hemlock (an extremely poisonous plant, from the parsley family, that can result in death) didn't live to describe its effects!

The discovery of remedies for different ailments emerged from these first experiments, with varying degrees of success. For a long time, their recipes were known and passed down by only a chosen few, such as priests, druids, witches, or healers.

It wasn't until the nineteenth century, when enormous progress was made in chemistry, that various parts of plants, minerals, and even animals were extracted and combined for beneficial effect. And the first medicine was born.

Today, technological advances have allowed us not only to artificially reproduce what nature creates on its own, but also to invent new chemical compositions that are even more effective and less costly. This is what we call "synthetic chemistry."

Yet despite these scientific achievements, the majority of people from a number of countries in Asia, Africa, and South America continue to use traditional remedies aimed at maintaining the body's defenses, to prevent illness. Wouldn't it be ideal to combine these two kinds of medicine? That way, you could maintain good overall hygiene to ward off illness, but also take medicine to heal when illness does occur.

I have a stomachache!

Well, at least you no longer have a headache!

How can I obey orders?

"Don't do this! Don't do that!" Enough already! Parents, teachers, and coaches all have a way of giving orders—it's unbearable! So how can you learn to obey without gritting your teeth or rebelling? Well, there aren't a lot of different answers to this question. You simply have to understand why the orders are given in the first place!

The only time we should bow to authority is when it's respectable; in other words, when it's good for everyone. Therefore, we maintain the right to disobey anyone who is unjust. But be careful! This is not an invitation to systematically question everything asked of you!

Every society needs laws, and those laws must apply to everyone. Laws help maintain equality and respect for each individual. This is why the vast majority of us obey them without even thinking about it.

For example, a teacher is appreciated not because he's big and strong, but because he's fair. He maintains a kind of unwritten contract with his students based on mutual respect, in which everyone benefits. If he's unfair, punishes his students for no apparent reason, and randomly applies rules when it suits him, then obeying him would be impossible.

However, history has shown us how tyrants and dictators imposed laws serving their own ambitions and interests. This kind of rule is unacceptable, even if the people who lived under it had no choice but to keep quiet and submit to it. It is this kind of abuse of power that inevitably leads to war and hate.

How did April Fools' Day come about?

There are many theories regarding the origin of April Fools' Day, but they all reach the same conclusion: April Fools' is a day filled with pranks and jokes!

Until 1563, Easter, a Christian holiday commemorating the resurrection of Christ, marked the beginning of the calendar year. This day was determined by the religious calendar. But in an attempt to impose his authority, King Charles IX of France decided in 1564 that the beginning of the new year would move from April 1 to January 1.

Mark Twain once said, "April First: This is the day upon which we are reminded of what we are on the other three-hundred and sixty-four."

April Fools' Day is a great opportunity to play pranks on your family, but be careful about taking a joke too far! Use your judgment when deciding how to fool your friends and family, and try to make your pranks something that everyone can laugh at.

The people who clung to the old calendar system continued the exchange of gifts and money that normally occurred during the celebration of the new year. Easter happened to fall on April 1 that year. Eventually, the exchange of gifts transformed into "gag gifts," and, ultimately, jokes.

Some companies and media groups play April Fools' Day pranks as well. For example, Burger King once advertised that it had invented a "left-handed" hamburger, which had condiments that dripped out o the right side. Lots of Internet pranks are pulled on April Fools' Day as well.

How do we remember things?

Try to picture your brain as a gigantic network of nerve endings, almost like an electrical circuit filled with wires. This network is made up of numerous nerve cells called neurons. Neurons are connected to one another through synapses.

Each time we learn something new, this information flows through our nervous system by way of synapses and neurons. When we repeat the same lesson ten different times, the information always takes the same route.

The sound of a door slamming shut remains in our memory for only a few thousandths of a second. The memory of the face of a person we pass on the street stays with us for about several seconds. If we don't make any effort to recall it, we simply forget it.

That's why siblings, even though they grow up under the same roof and share similar experiences, don't always have the same memories. In fact, people retain only those things in life that have marked them personally.

Who are you again?

Oh, right, you're my daughter.

Silly me!

After the one hundredth time, the route between neurons and synapses has been covered so many times that we end up memorizing the lesson by heart. It's stocked in our memory. But how long will it remain there?

On the other hand, the words and gestures we've learned over the years, the faces and places we love, and the most significant moments in our lives stay in our memory for a long time.

Index
by subject

Living Together

Life

Feelings

And More . . .